Pip the Kitten

by Karra McFarlane

illustrated by Hannah McCaffery

OXFORD
UNIVERSITY PRESS
AUSTRALIA & NEW ZEALAND

It is Pip.

Pip tips a tin.

Sam is mad.

Pip nips a map.

Dad is mad.

A nap in a pan.

Tim is mad.

Pip is sad.

Dad pats Pip.

Sam and Tim pat Pip.